MW01172920

THE SEVEN O'CLOCK BELL

Philip O Hunte Dip.MA

THE SEVEN O'CLOCK BELL

Copyright © 2017 by Philip O Hunte

Hunte, Philip
The Seven O'clock Bell

ISBN 13: 978-1543120684
ISBN-10: 1543120687

Printed in the United States of America

Dedicated to my mother, Mrs Ordene Beckles, my grandmother Mrs Adelaide Haynes, Angela, my wife, Dr Kari Hunte and Kristin, my daughters.

Perspectives of plantation life in the 1960's have indelibly etched a mark in my mind, sensitizing me to that harsh phenomenon of racism, which has blighted and discriminated globally against people of African descent.

Justice, in my estimation, is when people of all races are treated equally, without the brutal discrimination. A condition in which all are happy with fair play and righteousness.

My compliments to Trevor G Marshall for editing this book - vignettes of social conditions of contemporary plantation life.

So he who had received five talents came and brought five other talents, saying, 'Lord, you delivered to me five talents; look, I have gained five more talents besides them.' His lord said to him, 'Well done, good and faithful servant; you were faithful over a few things, I will make you ruler over many things. Enter into the joy of your lord.'

Jesus the Messiah,

(Matthew 25:20-21)

Contents

INTRODUCTION

Nestled in the north-east of the parish of St. George on Highway 3B, abutting and abounding Golden Ridge pumping station on the border of St. John, and abutting and abounding Lemon Arbor village, lies Ashbury plantation. This area comprises 420 acres of fertile agricultural land on the south of the highway, and the former tenantry to the north. Ashbury plantation has been the theatre of a mélange of activities, both social and economic, from the seventeenth century, just after the British colonizers settled Barbados. Its ownership has changed hands on several occasions since this historical event.

Ashbury has been a significant bargaining chip for the European and British sugar moguls and power brokers. This discourse seeks to encapsulate and give a synopsis of the social events and conditions which existed in the nineteen sixties and early seventies. However, it would be remiss of me to look at these without giving a chronology of the ownership succession and juggling which took place from the seventeenth century until the year 1970, when the present incumbent assumed ownership of this plantation.

Historical documents show that in 1674, Ashbury was owned by Messer's Horne and Husbands. Horne died in 1679 while heavily indebted. His co-owner, Samuel Husbands, married Elizabeth Horne, nee Holdipp. Husbands and his new wife took possession of the plantation, to which Elizabeth Horne had dower rights of one–third land and stock. Husbands also has dower rights and agreed to pay Colonel Horne's debts totalling

10,735 pounds sterling, of which 526,829 pounds, avoirdupois, of muscavado sugar, valued at 12 shillings per hundredweight or a total of 3,292 pounds sterling, formed as part. He also undertook to lease the plantation works and slaves for seven years, at one hundred and twenty pounds per year, from Colonel John Horne's son, Thomas Horne, in lieu of 420 acres.

In 1721, one Gohier, a London merchant and his son James Gohier, domiciled in Barbados. Through a series of transactions, they sold the plantation with three bond servants and 246 slaves, the total value of the slaves being 3,162 pounds sterling. A series of transactions transpired in which Ashbury was bought by John Nurse, also the owner of the adjacent Todds plantation, for seventeen thousand pounds sterling. The subsequent years were turbulent until 1806, when John Nurse paid Van Homigh, a Dutchman, 7,250 pounds sterling representing capital and interest of a mortgage by Francis Bell and William Forbes, which Forbes had assigned to Van Homigh. Following a Petition to the House, John Bell, descended from an ancient respectable family, took ownership of the plantation.

One Judge Bell, his relative, died in 1760, when John was 8 years old. Educated in England, John returned to Barbados at age 21, was married and was placed in possession of Lemon Arbor plantation, comprising 137 acres and 85 slaves. This plantation was encumbered with legacies of 5,000 pounds sterling, besides annuities and debts due to a tradesman. The hurricane of 1780 added to John Bell's difficulties. This hurricane was indeed one of the harshest hurricanes, resulting in wide-scale damage and financial losses to the planter class, as well as several human casualties.

Thus the plantation changed hands between wealthy landowners and absentee planters throughout the 18th century, to pay debts, with slaves constantly being re-owned and being sold off as part of deals for debt payments. The plantation was used for mortgage payment by the wealthy. In 1768 it belonged to William Forbes who mortgaged it to James Ballmere of London to secure 300 pounds, which was increased by 1,200 pounds in 1772 for further advance by Ballmere.

In 1773, Francis Bell purchased the plantation. Forbes gave him a mortgage of 11,270 pounds sterling. In 1774, Forbes assigned the debt to Ballmere for 11,482 pounds sterling.

In 1774, Ballmere and Forbes assigned a mortgage to Balthazar Van Homigh of Amsterdam city. In 1778, Horne was levied by J. Pieterjohn, as attorney for Van Homigh. The sum of money due Van Homigh was 8,250 pounds sterling. As a result of indebtedness, on 18th October 1784, the marshal executed absolute sale to Samuel Reece.

By 1802, John Nourse purchased Ashbury and Todds plantations for 17,000 pounds sterling total value. The Nourses owned these till 1898. Colonel L. Nourse owned the plantation from 1901-1907 as absentee owner. Colonel A.H. Nourse succeeded from 1912-1921. L Nourse et. al from 1929-1937, 1951-1957. L.T, H.E, R.H. Nourse and R.E Gill from 1957-1958. R.E Gill was deceased in 1970 and the plantation bequeathed to his estate; present owner is Michael Gill. A series of lawsuits had been brought against successive owners.

Ashbury is a big plantation with large fertile canefields, each of which had a name assigned to them: Baller, Ramsey, Chiggery, Lime Kiln. At its peak in the sixties, all were under sugarcane cultivation. In those days, sugar plantations were obligated to allocate 12 percent of their acreage to the production of foodstuffs; hence there was the proliferation of sweet potatoes, yams, and eddoes. The concept of 'food security' had a lot more currency in the sixties as people had to be more self-sufficient out of sheer necessity.

The undulating canefields of verdant hue were a sight to behold, moreso when the crop was flowering or in arrows which had a silver hue. Well-kept fields bordered by khus khus grass, which not only served to prevent soil erosion, but the blades of which were used for stuffing pillows, or for the bleaching of clothes in the sun. The roots were used for making khus khus perfume. In the sixties, fragrances like Estee Lauder, Givenchy, Elizabeth Arden were unheard of.

1

WORKING CONDITIONS

The bell in the plantation yard would toll at 6:45 a.m. to remind workers that work time was near. It would toll again at 7:00 am. These were roll calls for all the 'hewers of sugarcane and drawers of water' to be galvanized into action. Women were normally bedecked in cotton clothing, blouses and shirts, and sometimes in pants and crocus bags around their waistlines. Men were normally clothed in thick, sometimes patched, khaki pants and shirts with their sa-pax, an indigenous pair of sandals made from tyres. They would hustle to the plantation yard, then would scurry through the cartroads to the plantation yard to work until they were laid off at 4.30 p.m. These groups were assigned to 'gangs' to dig cane holes, fork, weed, clear hedgerows or cut horse dung. This was an organic fertilizer, a lot more potent than modern, synthetic fertilisers. In the crop season, the main métier would be cutting and loading canes.

There was a division of labour among these groups. There was the driver, or supervisor in modern parlance. He was a privileged individual. He did not have to indulge in the backbreaking métiers like the field workers and he had more recognition than them. The truck drivers were also privileged in that they received higher wages, and did not have to indulge in back breaking work. He could cool out in the canefields until the trucks were fully laden with canes, drive the truck to Uplands factory, where the cane would be weighed, unloaded by the hoist, receive the weight tickets, indicating the tonnage of the canes, which would have been a determinant of the wages of the cutters and the loaders, make the journey back to the canefied to await another load. Their children were the 'social darlings' of the plantation. Their families could afford luxuries which the normal 'field nigga' could not afford.

One could not imagine how these men and women toiled under such backbreaking conditions from 7:30 am til 4:30 pm, with one hour for lunch, breakfast as it was called at the time, with no rest rooms, cumbersomely dressed in khaki and flannels and sa-pax or guttarperks and pumps and socks, unwittingly enriching massa. Although they were not owned physically, they were to all intents and purposes under his control. Many had worked on weekends to construct the overseers house, for next to nothing, yet this is the same overseer who was quoted to have said that whites should never do nothing for a "nigger".

The 'heartman' was a dreaded bogey man. Every year in the Michaelmas term, one was told that the heartman was out, and in an environment surrounded by canefields, this placed fear and trepidation in the hearts of many a child. St. George was the parish with the reputation for 'devil men'. Two reputable shopkeepers had been deemed as devil men, hence the anxiety of many a youth! Young children would scurry along the cartroads to and from school. No wonder that some had athletic propensities.

The bell would toll again at 11.00 a.m. to signal lunch time. In actuality it was commonly known as breakfast time. Men and women would have their lunches brought into the cane piece, usually by the older girls, many of whom prepared these meals and were unemployed. Some would come home for a bite.

Lunch was simple, consisting of ground provisions, yams, sweet potatoes, eddoes, dumplings, cou cou, salt meat soup, cod fish or red herring gravy with Clover Queen butter usually washed down with mauby or lemonade. Sometimes the teenage boys and girls would assist their parents in loading a breadth of canes.

The third class persisted until the nineteen-sixties, a system in which the young had to assist their parents on the plantation. Their tasks included, cutting pond grass, weeding, hoeing, helping to load a breadth of canes in the boiling sun. It was a slave-like and iniquitous system which many parents vowed never to let their children work under. It was only after the democratization of education in 1962 that this exploitative regime ceased. Many an enterprising youth found his ambitions and academic dreams, and the chances of social mobility at the time, dashed as a result of this imposition.

The environment on the plantation was a far cry from what it is today. Sugarcane dominated the landscape and by extension the economy. The concept of 'economic diabetes' could be applied to Barbados, where the dominance of sugar was a malignancy to the rest of economic life and society, having a debilitating effect on most of the populace. In the rural areas where blatant social and physical oppression still prevailed, residents were bound in a yoke of deprivation, and a vicious cycle of poverty.

Ashbury's population stock was comprised of two families. At the turn of the twentieth century, they had moved to the plantation from the neighbouring parish of St. John to find employment, Opportunities to find work especially by the unskilled were at a premium. There was always the possibility of incestuous relationships being formed, as might have been the case in some instances. Contemporary sixties families were the Devonishes, the Hayneses, the Innisses, the Paynes, the Walcotts, the Harewoods. All of these families were derived from the original stock from St. John. Although separate, a deep look into their genealogies would indicate some connection from the original families, but through marriage and the subsequent name changes the familial divisions became a reality.

2

SOCIAL SYSTEM

A hierarchical system still existed on the plantation in the sixties. It was Massa's construct and served his purpose. There was the house nigga and the field nigga. The house 'niggas' cooked massa's food and were the nannies of his children. They were entitled to certain privileges and not exposed to the daily grind in the broiling sun. Their bodies did not undergo the wear and tear of the field niggas, and many of them lived to a ripe old age. The field niggas were the truck drivers, the canecutters and loaders, and the drivers, who were essentially the supervisors. Adults used to address the overseer's children as Ms. Rose and Ms. Ruth, Massa had an Austin Cambridge and kept small breed dogs which would run alongside the car and even attempt to scare away young children who passed through the plantation or low yard as it was referred to at the time. 'The Massas' also kept German Shepherds, Alsatians, Bulldogs and the silent Doberman Pinschers.

His children were well dressed and attended private schools. Massa subdivided one of his canefields among six of the plantation workers, men. The plots were of approximately half acre in area. They were not required to pay rent for these plots, and these were used to grow vegetables, namely, cabbages, cassava, yams, sweet potatoes, lima beans, bonavis, vegetable marrow, and finger squash and a plethora of other crops. These crops were used to supplement the nutritional requirements of families. Also, some of the men had milch cows and the 'cow pens' were one of the features which decorated some of these plots of land. From these came pen manure which was a very good organic fertilizer, predating the synthetic fertilizer currently in widespread use around the country.

Many of the residents manifested a virulent inferiority complex. 'Cuss outs' were a common feature, with many strained relationships. Some of the womenfolk in particular would lift their skirts above their heads inviting others to parts of their anatomies in the vilest of terms. They were unaware of who was their true enemy and oppressor, or their purpose for creation. As a consequence, there was a real ingrained envy and jealousy among them as could be seen in the fights even at the standpipe. Many of the residents were not on speaking terms, till death.

Most of the residents could not attend church as they did not have 'church clothes'. The Anglican Church, the established church under Bindley Brathwaite, made it mandatory that churchgoers had to be well clad, with the women covering their heads. Thus, the leading denomination did not welcome the lower classes at the time. It would have been a colossal embarrassment for anyone to attempt to enter the Anglican church without decent-looking clothes and shoes. Also at this time the Anglican church did not christen many of the babies who were born out of wedlock. They were referred to as 'bastards' and basically had no status or to some extent, rights of inheritance to property as did their brothers and sisters born in wedlock. Common law relations as now were the norm. The christening of these children was the métier of the Methodists Church and other denominations. It was only after legislation was passed to regularize the status of children born out of wedlock that this anomaly was corrected.

The spiritual needs of most of the residents were looked after by the revivalist movements which held spot meetings at certain strategic points outside the homes of individuals who opened their houses or allowed them to host services. The traditional cymbals, the clapping of hands, getting in the spirit when the Holy Ghost entered them, and speaking in tongues, a language which only the speaker could decipher. Participants would occasionally give donations, as there were no churches to support, and albeit the gatherings were small.

Everyone on the plantation had a nickname often determined by their physical appearance or by their antics and mannerisms. There was Donkey, Baa Wax, Terogee, Gearbox, Ossie Moore (not the original one, but a character who used to talk a lot of foolishness), Sprigdee , Grub, Abbott, Pookie, SP, Sample, Scar, Raggie, Jessie James, Colin Maughie, Gully Boar and Mock Police, Carl Lucy and Jessie.

There was a type of bantering which is visibly absent in modern Barbados, especially when it was time to pick coconuts in the low yard. The older boys used to delight in initiating girls. They would spend endless hours targeting nubile females who showed any signs of receptivity. Some were more fortunate, while others had to wait their turn. In those days they weren't many signs of courtship, and many of the parents did not 'want' certain individuals for their children, especially the girls, thus many were forced to do things secretly.

For games, the young played hop scotch, marble or kneel down cricket, pitched marbles, played cricket in the road with knit balls and rubberline compass balls, and with bats made from coconut branches or bits of wood. There were no playing fields then as is now. We played behind the water reservoir of Golden Ridge, the only green space in the area, in the plantation 'low yard', or in the tar road. This was the local parlance for the highway. The roads were made of stone, as a foundation, and on this was laid layers of bitumen. These were obviously narrow and of rough construction. In those days, vehicular traffic was very few. Many could not own a car, except an old Ford Jalopy of early sixties vintage. If memory serves right, no one in Ashbury plantation owned cars, except for those of the overseer, an Austin Cambridge and the bookkeeper whose car was an Austin of England 8.

The low yard as we coined it was 'Massas' preserve. It was a wide expanse of paved land stretching from the overseer's and bookkeeper's quarters' and into the orchard where the older men at the turn of the century had cultivated hog plums, chilli plums, bajan cherries, the ubiquitous guavas and coconuts. A road linked these buildings which were of stone construction. The low yard was a thoroughfare for children going to St. Judes School and also for churchgoers until the present owner Michael Gill debarred access to this area when he assumed ownership of the plantation in 1970.

This fruit orchard and a large area cultivated with coconut trees which my grandfather had related to me in the twilight of his days that they had planted at the turn of the twentieth century. Thus somehow this area was regarded as common property, as we had access to an abundance of fruit. In those days, the roads were of the type of several years vintage. The roads were only paved in 1965. In those days, vehicular traffic was no way as frequent as today. You could play a game of cricket uninterrupted by vehicular traffic. Also, at that juncture, the dismal lack of social amenities like playing fields and green spaces were unheard of, even as it is the case in many rural districts today. The older boys would catch fish in, the low yard tank. Their catches were usually hundreds or tilapia, which they would be keep in glass jars, Andrews swamp or in Tappy Pond, near to Redland Plantation. There was a close relationship among the residents of Ashbury, Golden Ridge, Superlative and St. Judes, almost everyone knew each other and in many cases, some were related.

The older men would take the weekend trek to Archie Holder's shop, now, Vic Wagon's Wheel, or Ms. Greene's, Doctor the butcher's shop in St. Jude's to drink rum. Sucking canes was a pastime of all and in many cases along with fruit from the gully, was a valuable nutritional supplement. Boys would regularly go into the canefields and suck frozen joys or juicees, 151's, B47's and many could be seen heading home heaps of these sugary supplements for later consumption. The present sugar industry is a skeleton of the past. Large open spaces were to be found in the canefields, the result of these raids, though occasionally there were the result of the nuptial rendezvous for young boys and girls.

The young had chores and these would be determined by gender. Looking after the stocks, sheep, pigs, yardfowls, ducks, rabbits milking the cows, the occasional goat, were all part of the daily routine before and after school. The girls cleaned the houses, washed, starched with arrowroot, starch ironed with flat clothes irons, even for their parents in association with the mothers who sometimes had these chores, even after eight hours in the boiling sun.

The concept of the Yardfowl was a prominent feature. Almost every household possessed these chickens. These were a free ranging birds and would nest in the trees, and the nearby vegetation and were very hard to domesticate. They would roost at nights in a procession which commenced with failing light. They were omnivorous, eating mice, cockroaches, lizards even phlegm from peoples' noses, and their owners would also feed them cracked corn, scratch grain and bun bun, burnt food from their pots, usually rice or ground provisions. Yardfowls usually laid their eggs in the bushes or under the house cellars and after three weeks of sitting on their clutches would emerge with their very attractive broods which could be as many as ten in some instances. One could always tell when a hen laid as she would go off into a wild cackle. To stop hens from 'laying out' that is laying in the bushes, sometimes, one was required to feel the fowl, that is perform a digital examination to see if a ripe egg was there, in which case the hen was impounded in the fowl coop. The next day one was assured that there were more eggs in the household.

Yardfowl meat was the main item on the excursion menu. You would behead three or four of them, and bake them. The church excursion or outing was an expedition to the more remote parishes in Barbados, St. Lucy and St. Peter were the main rendezvous. Archers and River Bay in St. Lucy and the Animal Flower Cave and Half Moon Fort. Sunday School children, by dint of their contributions, usually as little as five cents per week would be issued with a ticket. The cost at the time never exceeded seventy-five cents. Adults paid two dollars for their tickets. We would be driven to St. Jude's Village where all the residents of the environs would board the traditional Bajan buses, running board and all, for our journey to these remote destinations. We enjoyed the trip, beating the sides of the buses and singing some of the Bajan folksongs, some not so wholesome.

On the eve of this event, adults would stay awake till early morning, making sandwiches, baking the yardfowls and pork. Yardfowl meat was a bit tougher, as these birds were wandering 'free range' and not confined to coops and force fed. It had a distinctly stronger flavor. The yardfowl could be a source of contention as sometimes they ended up the wrong baskets or in the neighbour's pot. The crow of the cock at foreday morning was an indication of a new day. Several residents started their day at the clarion crow of the cocks at first light, and this would set off a cacophony of sound among other cocks in the district, as though they were trying to outdo each other.

Residents of Ashbury had few or no social amenities through which they could relax from the daily grind on the plantation and vent their pent up energies and frustrations. Men drank rum, played dominoes and cards, gambled and went home and impregnated their spouses. The women worked hard in the fields, went home and looked after their families. There were occasional dances in St. Judes Primary School, Gall Hill Social Centre in St. John and at Charles Row Bridge. In those days, fifty or seventy cents could get you on a dance floor. Some of the more free spirited residents attended these social events.

Rum and coke, beers, pork chops, black pudding and souse were the main fare. This was the era of the juke box, and in the late sixties, the record player with the vinyl records of 33 1/3,

45 and 78 rpm. This was the era of pointed tip shoes, pipe bottom and gun mouth pants, and crew cut hairstyles, succeeded by Afro hairstyles and the Black Power salute. During the latter part of the sixties with the advent of the Black Power movement and Black consciousness, such soul singers as Otis Redding, Percy Sledge, Solomon Burke, Wilson Pickett, Joe Tex, Aretha Franklin, The Supremes and regionally. In terms of calypso, The Mighty Sparrow, Kitchener and Lord Melody dominated the airwaves. The 'Service of Song' was also another social event which was hosted by more of the socially conscious and popular members of the community.

Parents could not afford modern toys and thus many boys and girls were very innovative. Rollers were constructed from bicycle wheels from which the spokes had been removed, also from car parts, scooters, tractors and trucks to duplicate activities on the plantation, using milk tots and sardine pans. Girls used to keep house, a training ground for their maternal roles. They also used cloth dolls, and 'Mock Men' from cloth and at Christmas 'Father Christmas'. We would erect a cloth man or as some would say a mock man and hurl or pelt him with stones.

Games included hitty-bitty shut up your lap, puss catch a corner, pitching marbles, marble or kneel down cricket. Bats were made from the branches of coconut trees which were all pervasive in the plantation yard, also knit balls, which required a unique skill using a needle and twine, rubber strand balls from bicycle inner tubes again an improvised and unique skill. Wherever the twos and threes were gathered, a game of cricket would start. Cricketers used to pick sides opposing teams, tip and run firms, whenever you struck a ball you had to attempt a run, hence several run outs also tip a two, whenever you struck a ball you had to attempt two runs, and last man bat out where you had to capture all the wickets of your opponents. Cricket was played in the tar road in the cart roads which separated the canefields or in the grass pieces of sour grass. There were few interruptions, as in those days there were hardly any motor vehicular traffic in the rural districts and these venues proved to be more than adequate for growing boys.

The plantation was served by one shop, the two door peddling shop. The owner, my grandmother, was a woman of valour who had migrated from Trinidad at the age of four. Her mother was a schoolteacher, a vocation which she herself had intentions of pursuing, but due to economic hardship was forced to become a servant, maid, baker, bread seller and finally, a small shopkeeper. This shopkeeper would extend credit to the residents. Men would credit cigarettes and coca colas. She did not sell alcohol. On many occasions, creditors would run up credit and not honour it, stop patronizing her, when they thought she forgot, would come again and run up new credit. She and her offspring could have been better off financially if she had been less generous to the poor masses of people to whom, out of her altruistic nature, she gave sometimes her last.

She sold most of the consumer goods which a poor impoverished consumers could demand even if not afford in the sixties. Basic goods like rice, flour, sugar, macaroni, codfish, red herrings, sardines, salt meat, neck ribs, snout, flat ribs, and pigtail. Also there was barley, oats, sago, tea, coffee, Milo and Ovaltine. Some families could afford to treat themselves with herring in tomato sauce, mackerel and corned beef. This was a three pot era even if it included two servings of rice. Alarmingly there were few signs of malnutrition.

Residents had access to yams, potatoes and eddoes which were planted on the plantation and also the plots of the men who were fortunate enough to be granted these half acre plots by 'massa'. As then, moreso than today, the ubiquitous breadfruit tree adorned almost every home. It was a staple crop for making breadfruit cou cou, steaming as in stew food, with cassavas, sweet potatoes, yams, dumplings, strethched out, that is when it was cut into large slices and not processed as in pickled souse. It was a very versatile fruit, allowing for several ways of its preparation. The soft ones were fed to pigs or slightly cooked and sold to ducks and chickens.

There was the spectre of abject poverty among some of the residents. Many were condemned into being enforced vegetarians. Sometimes they could not afford any type of meat. Mustard bush and rice or okra leaves and rice were the menu items in some instances. But, there were no signs of malnutrition, as there were bountiful supplies of fruit, hog and chilli plums, bajan cherries, golden apples, pink and white flesh guavas, star apples and mammy apples which were in bountiful supply in the nearby St. Judes graveyard, which we passed on our daily trek to St. Judes School. Additionally, Massa had granted half acre plots to some of the male labourers on which they planted provisions to augment the food of their families, and some to share with residents. It was not a difficult task to take plantation produce and some were seen heading home with bags of potatoes and yams and would take the produce of those workers who had been granted their half acre plots.

By the end of the decade of the sixties, the bell was tolling on the one-door shops, with the advent of the Cash N' Carries and the supermarkets. It was no longer economically viable to run a small shop; many of the customers had become more affluent or could not be seen at these small establishments. There had been a fall-off in her customer base. Some of her neighbours in the district had never patronized her shop for even the basic products and with the advent of The Cash N' Carry and the Shamrock, some arrogantly boasted that they no longer shopped at two-door shops. Despite their idle boast when things got hard they came to credit, and she, through her benevolence, extended this facility to them. Put succinctly, things got hard towards the end of the sixties. In Bajan parlance, the sow had 'gotten under the counter'.

The itinerant bread seller from the nearby village of Superlative would travel from her domicile, two days a week, tray on her head and her Mauby pail. Her fare would include pone, flour and corn, turnovers, sweetbread, both hard and soft which she did through the kneading process. She would extend credit to the labourers, especially those who were unable to prepare such would credit their lunches from her. Also the black pudding and souse woman would travel from St. Judes on Saturday mornings with her fare. Freshly cut parsley and seasoning and onions. These foods were quite inexpensive, but many were unable to afford the good stuff. In general, the food in those days tended to be more delicious, because the soils in which the prime staples, yams, potatoes, eddoes were grown were arguably more fertile than these which exist today. The pork, lamb and beef also was more tasty, perhaps as a result of the simple and hygienic way of keeping and feeding the livestock, from swill, scraps of food, corn, animal feed sour and elephant grass and sugarcane tops which were very plentiful during the crop season.

3

HARD TIMES

This was the whole tenor of life on the plantation. It was particularly accentuated at the end of the crop season. The lyrical master, Red Plastic Bag, in one of his classic calypsos, "Mr. Harding" alluded to this phenomenon. Life on the plantation was always one of "hard times', especially after the close of the crop season. Workers were given three days' work, usually weeding, hoeing, cutting cane butts, ratoons to plant out rested fields, this was referred to as supplying their canes and ensured high cane yields of future years. Raking trash which was a mulch, transporting fertilizer from the port to the plantation yard, and this at that was done manually. In those days it was usually a case of fish manure, sulphate of ammonia or potash. Take home pay was on average about fifteen dollars a week. It was only towards the end of the sixties when some workers were unionized, that wages rose above fifty dollars a week, and this was during the sugar harvest.

It was miraculous how plantation folk survived under these straitened economic and financial conditions. Alarmingly there was no evidence of malnutrition. Protein was in short supply, but the bountiful supply of fruits from the low yard and from trees planted by the residents in close proximity to their dwelling places. The role played by the ubiquitous breadfruit cannot be underscore. Most houses were in close proximity to these 'wonder trees'. A ripe breadfruit could provide a meal for a family, but many youngsters could consume one, or even two of these wonder fruits when they were roasted. The roasting process consisted of starting a wood fire, from bits and pieces, placing breadfruits on top of this flame, and continuously placing more and more wood atop of these fruits. A roasted breadfruit when completely black from the carbon, is one form of best tasting breadfruit. A slight variation of the method of preparation was to place the breadfruit in a fire, you would cut the heart from the breadfruit and place a pre-prepared gravy, butter sauce, consisting of onions, Clover Queen Butter, placing the breadfruit this time upright. The gravy would permeate the meat of the breadfruit roasted in this format was easily the most flavourful.

Life in the sixties was quaint and simple for the people who eked out a living on Massa's land. There were no luxuries. Kitchen utensils included the monkey, used to store water. The conaree jar for storing meat, salt meat and codfish, then a giffen good, nevertheless a staple in the sixties were the main sources of protein. The original notion of touch pork, when the pork started to ferment with an odour, was a delicacy for the old men. The mortar and pestle were used for making seasoning and other condiments. The buck and coal pot were used for 'potting' pork, still the most delicious form of pork, a skill which has been lost to young Barbadians. Houses were essentially Bajan, the chattel variety, the movable wood frame one gable hut which was precariously perched on large or medium sized coral stones. This was a reflection of the insecurity of the plantation dwellers.

The front house, shed and kitchen, moreover the fire hearth, the stone fireplace where wood fires were ignited using wood, and coals to cook food on the coal pot. The houses were all of wood, temporary constructions, placed on limestone, or soil stone as it was commonly known. This was an adaptation to the fact not only that the residents could not afford more luxurious dwellings, but they did not have the title to the land on which they lived. Instead of threat of eviction, they paid a weekly nominal rent to the overseer for their tenure of their 'house spots' from the paltry wages which they received. Wages ranged from ten to fifteen dollars during the hard times, for a five day week and upwards to thirty five dollars during 'Crop Season'. Sometime in the late sixties, a three day week was enforced on some plantations, and in many cases take home pay for plantation workers was fifteen dollars.

Up to the sixties, the oil lamp and the occasional lantern were the main forms of light in the households at nights. Some folks were so poor that they used to improvise and use a 'bull or smut lamp', which essentially was an empty drink bottle filled with kerosene oil, with a piece of cloth which was ignited. This was a very hazardous form of light as the danger always existed of tripping on them and causing a fire. This can also be used as a Molotov cocktail. Thus it was a daily chore of having to clean lamp chimneys, trim wicks, fill lamps with kerosene and ignite lamps when night-time approached. Electricity came to Ashbury in 1970. Running water was introduced to Ashbury in 1963. Prior to this, residents headed water from the standpipe to their homes. The standpipe in itself was a social institution. It was a rendezvous where all congregated. It was a grapevine where the latest news and gossip was revealed. The standpipe was also the place where disputes were settled. Women could get a beating for gossip and backbiting or for horning, taking away another girl's fella.

The canefields were a source of food. Sucking canes was a hobby. It was almost instinctive to suck canes, and this practice contributed to the daily nutrition of many a boy. The canefield was also a toilet for many as in those days many had neither pit toilets and certainly not water toilets. Perhaps this was one of the reasons why among other things cane yields were so high as compared with today. Also the canfield was a bedroom, a place for intimacy, where consulting adults and adolescents could obtain their sexual gratification. Many were probably conceived in the canefields and cartroads of the plantation.

The old folk knew about the old herbs and bushes. There was Christmas bush, cerasee, epie, gullyroot, which the Jamaicans now call guinea Hen Bush, and claim it as their own, with all of its curative qualities for cancer. Garden and rock balsam, clammy cherry, cooling bushes, for hot nights. Governor ball, black sage, oil leaves from the wild castor oil plant which was used to sweat heads in bouts of head colds. Also dog dumplings, now known as Noni, and noted for its curative qualities in cancer fighting and a plethora of old bushes, known to the old generation, and no longer at our disposal.

Old men worked in the fields, weeding, cutting hedgerows of khus khus grass, digging cane holes for which they were paid a few cents per hole. It was necessary to work hard for Massa. My grandfather after having worked for fifty years on the plantation, had the proceeds of the sale of a heifer and an old house in his latter days. This was the sum total of his tiring and sustained effort for Massa. Many of these old men, though lacked ambition, and those who had, through economic necessity, were tied into a cycle of poverty. Inadequate education, low income, large families, poor nutrition and this cycle seemed at the time to be unbreakable.

The women in most instances contributed disproportionately to the upkeep of the households. In many instances, they actually owned the houses. They, of necessity had to be strong. In addition to domestic duties, they worked in the fields and endured many pregnancies. It was common at the time to have large families. The mean number being about five children, but it is recalled that one family had eleven offspring, including two twins, all surviving to adulthood. One couple had two sons in a calendar year. It would seem as though the biological law guaranteeing the survival of the species through large numbers was applicable.

In the early years of the sixties, the provision of health care was a rare service. Many of the older folk were stricken by chronic diseases, like high blood pressure, diabetes, strokes, arthritis and a myriad of other diseases. Many of these diseases were undiagnosed. It is only in retrospect that one can see that the physical appearances pointed to these diseases. Many of the men showed signs of hernia which was commonly referred to as goadies. One would hear so and so was sick. Then the infirmary or the alms-house as it was known then, and after a brief illness death, usually with an unceremonious departure. It was only in 1967 with the introduction of the National Insurance Scheme that workers received some semblance of social security and insurance to cover them in times of illness.

The working class people of Ashbury never shared in the vast wealth which sugar generated in the sixties. During these years, sugar production was consistently in the 150,000 tonne range. The union did not play an important role in those early days and, it was only after unionization that some of the workers began to receive a trickle down of some of the wealth. During one year of a windfall, one union boss retorted that they could not allow the union workers to have access to all of these large funds for them to eat it out, drink it out and piss it out. Wages were painfully low. It was possible to earn twenty dollars a week during the crop season after having hewed tons of canes during that period. Some workers were unable to calculate their earnings and hence took what they received. During the hard times, these could be seven dollars, from which a deduction for your house spot was made.

4

CROP SEASON

Crop time was the imaginary 'spring time'. All the sugar workers would literally spring to life with expectancy, more money was the main motivator. An increase in energy was needed to hew the large fields of sugarcane. Men would sharpen their bills, collins' and swords to chop the bounteous crops. Everyone was fit. This was not the job for the fat and the obese. With the clang of the bell, men and women would assemble in the plantation yard to be ushered to the designated canefield which in most cases had the ripest canes. Every canecutter would have a 'break' of cane, the women their loaders would load out a 'break'. Sometimes the quicker workers would assist the stragglers.

Men would race, cut the canes as fast as they could mainly for bragging rights, but this resulted in higher wages to the workers could cut the most and also their loaders. The women were the beast of burden. They worked in the fields and had to go home to their families and perform their other tasks. It was a puzzle as to how they managed to juggle roles. They headed canes to the truck, by bundles. Their neck muscles had to be very strong. It was a continuous and strenuous activity to get canes to Uplands sugar factory, long since mothballed would grind the thousands of tons of sugarcanes. The familiar scent of the steaming up for the commencement of the crop. The traditional delivery of the first canes. The boilers and the blowing of the factory horn meant that the crop season was ready to commence. The equipment had to be in ship shape. At full capacity, it was estimated had Uplands factory had the capacity to grind upwards to seventy tons of canes per hour. The sweet smell of the crack liquor permeated the air. The factory ash from the limestone used for purifying the cane juice would fall on the roofs of the houses.

Bulk sugar trucks, Bedfords, Austins, Morrises and Commers would make their way along the tar roads with this precious commodity, the backbone of the Barbadian economy at that juncture in time. At the peak of production, some trucks would make up to ten trips a day from Uplands to the terminal at the Deep Water Harbour for storage and subsequent shipment to the mother country. The more athletic boys would hop or hitch a ride on the trucks whilst some would chase these trucks until they got into high gear and proved too fast to pursue. By all standards, the drivers of these vehicles were handsomely paid for their labour. Also, molasses the residue from the crystallising of sugar, was used for the manufacture of rum, sweets, as a food in itself alcohol. These products were headed to the Deep Water Harbour for shipment to England, still the mother country.

5

SIGNS OF CHANGE

The abject poverty served as a motivator to many of the younger generation. There was that yearning to escape firstly the physical environment with its grinding poverty, but also not to be victim to the same social conditions which their parents and grandparents had endured. During the latter half of the sixties there was a mass exodus of young people from Ashbury. They migrated to the UK to do myriad of jobs such as nursing, conductors, bus drivers and chain shops, to Bermuda as a police and to the USA where they could improve their economic status, earn better paying jobs and some realize their real purposes in life.

Free Education in 1962 implemented by Errol Walton Barrow, premier from 1961 to 1966 and prime minister from 1966 to 1976 and again from 1986-1987, had served as a catalyst for this exodus from the plantation. For the first time children with academic potential could have a free education, if they so desired without burdening their parents. Some had received half scholarships, but prior to this many stopped school at age fourteen in class seven. Private secondary schools like the Modern High, Lynch's Secondary, The Cooperative High, The Federal High, The Arlington High, Christ Church High, The Washington High and Metropolitan High offered half scholarships to some students but in many cases, parents were forced to pay full fees to guarantee their children an education. This was an onerous task for many parents, bearing in mind their abject poverty and the low wages which they received. Many potentially bright children were thus forced to forego a secondary education.

Free secondary education meant that for the first time, the brighter children were enabled to enter the hallowed bastions of education: The Lodge, Harrison College, Queen's College Combermere, St. Michael's and Foundation. The sons and daughters of agricultural labourers, maids and shopkeepers had a chance to rub shoulders with, and in some instances excel the children of lawyers, doctors, the plantocracy, the whites and the middleclass whose preserve it had been. Thanks to Errol Walton Barrow.

Credit and hire purchase facilities from mainstream businesses were inaccessible to plantation dwellers. To obtain credit, workers were forced to go through the plantation overseer who acted as an intermediary between themselves, Manning, Wilkinson and Challenor, Ash and Watson and Herbert Lumber Yard. The workers were given letters of credit to take to the managers of these capitalist enterprises, on agreed terms with subsequent deductions being made from their wages. Credit was usually required when house repairs were needed to replace siding boards, corrugated galvanise sheets for roofs or for a new coat of paint. Houses were often of gabled roofs with the jealousie windows with the usual painting scheme being brown or grey, which added to the stygian gloom of the plantation. Some of the more thrifty would use the proceeds from the sale of a pig or a cow to initiate house repairs.

The "coolie men", the itinerant Indian vendors from Bombay, now Mumbai and Calcutta, Kolkata and Bihar State, played a very important role in the upkeep and maintenance of the lifestyles of plantation dwellers. These male vendors, mainly with valises and sometimes on bicycles, would trade with these poor people as still is the practice today. Kara, Nakhuda, Kasoji, Nanan and Gandhi were some of the more prominent vendors on whom the plantation dwellers were more dependent. They would supply such items as linoleum or congoleum, the other name for the floors, plastic for covering the tables, materials to make blinds, dresses and pants lengths in addition to a whole range of kitchen utensils. Armed with their cards on which they made a tally of their credit advances. Their handwriting for the most part was illegible, and creditors would pay for items for protracted periods, all the while incurring more credit as their personal needs grew. Manning Wilkinson and Challenor, at the time, Cave Shepherd, Fogarty, Harrisons were all inaccessible to the majority of the denizens of Ashbury for obvious reasons.

In talking to many of the older men in Ashbury, one realized that many of them possessed talents and faculties which they never had the chance to develop or exploit. Among their ranks were rock blasters, saddle makers, men who had worked in shops and would have had some business acumen. One was a Master-mason who related that he had assisted in the construction of the furnace at Andrews Factory. But, lack of opportunity, in some cases ambition and motivation precluded their development. The plantation was the only avenue when stark economic reality came home, especially when they started to raise families. My grandfather, in his latter years revealed how he started to work at age seven, after his father had died prematurely, at age thirty-eight, leaving eight children and a wife, who subsequently had to depend on him and his siblings for her sustenance.

The Tenantry Freehold Purchase Act engineered under the stewardship of JMGM 'Tom' Adams, Prime Minister from 1976-1985, offered inestimable and unforeseen opportunities for the residents of Ashbury. For the first time they could own land. These 'de facto' squatters who had paid a nominal rent to the plantation owners were empowered for the first time. They could thus erect permanent structures, free from the threat of eviction. They had a piece of the rock. Land ownership has always been the basis of empowerment. It was the landed barons and aristocracy of the UK who comprised the landed gentry. The residents of Ashbury have miraculously transformed this once derelict, impoverished plantation tenantry into a modern Barbadian neighbourhood.

A visit to Ashbury today reveals a district which is a far cry from conditions in the sixties. Many permanent wall structures instead of chattel houses, with cars parked outside. The landscape has changed dramatically. King sugar can still be seen on the southern flanks of the neighbourhood, but these are more akin to their relatives, giant elephant grass and not the heavy, high sucrose content canes which enriched massa and were a joy to the pallets of many of us. The cartroads are gone. Access to the plantation yard is gone. Young people no longer have to go there. However, many of the older generation who had used the low yard as a thoroughfare to St. Judes Church were forced to use a longer route to go there, some by St. Judes bus from Newbury corner. The owner had closed the road for an unknown reason. Many now have motorcycles and cars and far fewer attend church.

The young generation now have bicycles, trendy clothes, and modern technological gadgets. They have unbridled access to schools, alas a service which some do not utilize. Many still indulge in the pastimes of some of their ancestors, gambling, drinking and more recently smoking pot. Many parents still do not instill or support their children in obtaining an education, which would give them an outside chance of success, and not only serve as a catalyst to escape the old mindset, but free them from the trammels of material and spiritual poverty which had plagued and to some extent enslaved their ancestors.

Many of the young are among those lost generations to whom we failed to pass on truly Barbadian cultural traits and way of life. Their socialization has been fractured. The frenzy to flee from the trammels of material and spiritual poverty forced many to abandon Ashbury at the earliest opportunity. This social reality created a vacuum in this village which cannot be easily filled. Many of us don't have the time or don't care about mending that breach. A huge generation gap exists, with third and fourth generation descendants of the original population stock now living in the same spots of their ancestors. Materially, conditions have changed, but the lack of eagerness to capitalize on educational opportunities and the inability to enhance their skills has meant that socially, Ashbury is going full circle.

Despite all this, some of these old plantation folk were my heroes. They possessed few resources and were simple men and women who according to Genesis 3:19, by the sweat of their brows, they ate bread, raised their children as best they knew and could, and made their individual contributions to the development of Barbados. Unwittingly, they enriched the planter class, but this was out of dire economic necessity, a lack of insight and foresight and opportunity. To Gender, Donkey, Sea Bob or Buck Sheep or Tick Tick, Coppers, Julian, James Henry, Da Da, Albert, Bishop, Baby Douts, Coolie, Vangie, Eurie, Ilene, Adlin, that shopkeeper of valour, who raised her family and shielded us from the abject poverty of many of our neighbours, Sybil, Carmen et.al, congratulations! Your industry, resilience, tenacity and character must be acknowledged and celebrated!

ACKNOWLEDGEMENTS

Thanks to the Archives Department for allowing access to the C,E Queree documents, for which insight to the ownership patterns of Ashbury Plantation from the seventeeth century to the present were garnered.

About The Author

Philip Hunte was born on 4th December 1955 and was raised in Ashbury, which is a sugar plantation in St. George, Barbados. He attended St. Jude's Primary School (1960-1966), The Lodge School (1966-1973), and The Barbados Community College (1973-1975). He has worked as a civil-servant from 1976 until his retirement, while completing external studies with the Chartered Institute of Marketing, and Birmingham City University, UK.

Made in the USA
Columbia, SC
08 July 2022

63081089R00026